GET THE
BEST
OUT OF YOUR
PEOPLE
AND
YOURSELF

7 Practical Steps
for Top Performance

Val Williams

Executive Coach

Shadowbrook Publishing
P.O. Box 2458
Edison, New Jersey 08818

Second edition 2013

Library of Congress Control Number: 2001119743

ISBN 0-9712007-7-7

Dedicated to Dr. Bob Robison, who was the inspiration for this project. Thanks, Bob, for helping me become a better Executive Coach. Through our insightful conversations, I learned the age-old lesson: keep it simple. And yet, things that are simple are not always easy....

CONTENTS

ACKNOWLEDGEMENTS

Special thanks to my friend, Linda Manassee Buell, who showed me it was possible to write a book. Thanks to my book coach, Jim Donovan, who guided me through the many phases of creating a book that actually gets published. Thanks to my editors, Julie Lancaster and Linda Decker, who made my message clearer. Special thanks to my outstanding personal assistant, Marie Schulz, who does everything I need and is the backbone of my organizational success. Thanks to Thomas Leonard, founder of Coach University, who taught me the value of high-quality coaching. Thanks to my clients and friends, who added comments as real-life managers and executives. And most of all, thanks to my biggest fan, who encourages me endlessly, my husband, Randy Holmes.

FOREWORD

As someone who has spent most of his professional life developing and stressing the importance of leadership skills, I find this book to be an excellent, practical resource for managers. Each of these seven steps is an important leadership skill that many managers need but often don't spend enough time developing. Even when developed, these skills are often not used in a practical or effective way.

Val, in her writings, has captured the essence of staff development and the importance of providing timely and constructive feedback. Unfortunately, my experience has shown me that there are few how-to books on this subject that are easy to understand and simple to apply. This book has been able to accomplish both of these important goals.

Often times in American business we spend significant time teaching people technical skills specific to their assignments. Many times we do not spend enough time developing practical leadership skills in managers. Managing people is quite different from managing tasks. Therefore, I believe it is important to teach simple, practical steps that help identify and reinforce the key aspects of leadership. Managers will master one or two of these practical steps but have a difficult time developing all, and they need a resource that identifies the other important elements. This clear, simple-to-use and practical seven-step guide allows managers the ability to not only develop their own skills but to share those skills with other aspiring leaders within their organization.

I have found this book to be very helpful in my day-to-day business activities and I am certain that you, too, will want to apply these seven practical steps to your everyday business life. Leadership is the most important aspect of any corporate executives' role, and this book provides a significant foundation for developing the leadership skills important to success.

– Bertram L. Scott
CEO, TIAA-CREF Life Insurance

Bertram L. Scott is President and CEO of TIAA-CREF Life Insurance Company. For the past 20 years, he has worked in a variety of corporate leadership roles.

THE BIG PICTURE

Corporate America is a tough place. Being an executive or a manager is hard. I ought to know. I spent 13 years at a major insurance company, figuring out what it takes to be a great executive. And now, as an Executive Coach, I work every day with corporate managers and executives.

Managers and executives are under a lot of pressure these days. They need to produce valuable results for their companies—fast. They need to be inspirational leaders and great bosses. And they are stressed.

I understand why executives are stressed. Before starting my executive coaching business I was a healthcare executive. During my last executive job, I had a staff of more than 700 people in two locations with 12 managers reporting to me. Together we ran customer service operations in which we paid 2.8 million claims a year and answered 1.5 million phone calls a year. We were under the stress of having to pay 85% of these claims within 15 days and answer 85% of the phone calls within 30 seconds. And we did all this while hiring and training a growing staff, responding to sales force demands, managing a variety of human resource issues, and preparing audits and accreditations. For those of you who know the managed-care industry, it meant we often dealt with angry, frustrated people who wanted either their money or fast information. And the work mattered— It had a direct impact on people's hospitalizations and doctor visits.

Like most managers and executives in organizations, we managed all these people and did all this work during company reorganizations and rightsizing, in the midst of ongoing corporate politics. We managed our people while the industry was going through constant change, while running two shifts to keep up with new customer demands, and while feeling we had no outside life.

And through it all, you want to be a great manager. You are just trying to do good work so that you can continue being successful. Your staff members often ask you if their jobs are secure. Meanwhile, you worry day to day if your own job will be eliminated. And on top of all of this, you realize you had better get the best out of the people who report to you or you're dead!

I totally understand the pressure of being an executive. I "get" the stress involved in managing people. Whether you are a CEO, senior executive or line manager, one of the biggest challenges of management is:

How do you get people to be top performers? How do you, as a leader, manage your team so that your people grow and develop? How do you help your staff "rise to the occasion"—not just when there's a crisis, not just for a special project, but every day? In these days of constant change, turmoil and business demands: How do you get the best out of your people?

And when do you find time to develop people in the real world—where things move so fast you can't keep up, where email is overwhelming, where you don't know who your friends are, where multitasking is the norm? I've observed that executives and managers don't even have the time to read a book on "how." Executives are impatient. They need the short, executive summary, the "Cliff's Notes" of how to develop people.

That's why I wrote this handbook. Because as I coached busy executives, my clients just wanted the bottom line, the answers to their questions. And the questions were the same for many executives regardless of the industry, and regardless of their level:

- How do I get my staff to do what I want them to do?

- How do I push my direct reports to step up to the next level of performance?

- How do I use my power to get people to change their behavior?

- How do I communicate effectively enough so that I can have quick conversations to delegate work instead of doing things myself?

- How do I handle conflicts (since they happen a lot)?

So this handbook has no pretty prose, no poetry, no long philosophical explanations. This handbook is just the bottom line; because the solution for how to get the best out of your people is not a mystery. There are some practical and effective, common-sense approaches that work. If you are an executive or manager and you want to develop your people quickly, here are the things you should make sure you are doing.

The 7-Step Checklist

The core of this handbook is a checklist of seven key questions for people who manage people, and the solutions to those questions. The following checklist is the same one I use as an Executive Coach. I usually coach executives and managers with this checklist when they come to me with questions like, "How can I get my direct reports to perform at a higher level?" I ask each of the following questions and I look for the areas that need work.

If you want to develop people:

1. Are you setting clear enough <u>expectations</u> for your staff?

2. How often do you give your staff <u>feedback</u>?

3. What kinds of <u>conversations</u> do you have with people to develop them?

4. How well do you present <u>performance evaluations</u>?

5. How good a <u>delegator</u> are you?

6. How satisfied are you that you use <u>coaching skills</u>?

7. Do you <u>walk the talk</u>?

Then, depending on which area of this checklist is a concern, we go to work to develop the executive skill needed.

This handbook uses the term, "the manager." The manager could be at any level: a CEO, a vice president, a manager, or a supervisor—anyone who has direct reports. It also uses the term, "the employee" or "the staff." Again, this term could refer to employees at any level, from executive to line worker. The titles do not matter. We are just describing the role of the person who manages and the role of the person being managed. Interestingly, while coaching senior-level executives, I have learned that people-development skills are actually more important as you move higher up the corporate ladder. And as many vice presidents and chief officers know, sometimes you can reach very high executive levels without ever having been trained in the nuts and bolts of how to manage people's performance.

For example, many executives are promoted quickly due to their technical expertise. Then at the senior vice president level they find themselves without the skills to manage the high-level, experienced vice presidents that report to them. At executive levels, your direct reports do not need as much direct supervision. However, they have an even greater need for the leader's coaching and development. The stakes are higher. The results need to be bigger. And the higher you go in a corporation, the less you accomplish on your own, the more tasks are done by your people, and the less you can use authority to get people to do things. At higher levels, top leaders know that your main tool is "influence" vs. "authority." So how do you really influence people to be their best?

In this handbook you now have the 7-Step Checklist. The solutions to the seven key questions above are summarized in the following chapters. The chapters also include examples of real language for how a conversation would actually sound between the manager and employee. There are also quotes from real-life executives and managers who successfully manage people. I asked several executives and managers to share the most valuable lessons they have learned about different aspects of developing people. Their advice is wisdom from the real world.

At the end of each chapter is a "Manager's Action Plan." These are questions for you as the leader. This is where you evaluate your own performance in managing people and decide what actions you will need to take. Adapt the solutions to your own style. Use your own intuition. And most of all, start to actually enjoy the process of getting the best out of your people...and yourself.

STEP 1

SET CLEAR EXPECTATIONS

"Not everyone wants to be inspired.
Some people just want
clear instructions."

— *Greg Meyer*
Executive Coach

The first step in helping your staff deliver predict-able, high-level performance is to set crystal-clear expectations. Surprisingly, many managers skip this step. They assume the staff person knows what his or her job is, and what is expected, especially if the employee is a higher-level person. To make sure that expectations are clear, be sure you have the following in place:

- The employee has a written job description or summary of responsibilities. (Even at higher executive levels, a brief written scope of the job is useful.) In fact, when employees are at the manager level or above, they should write the job scope themselves.

- The manager has discussed this document with the employee and verified that the employee understands.

- Whenever job duties are changed, the written description is updated and discussed.

- The discussion of expectations should include not only the job requirements but also the manager's general expectations about the level of initiative expected from the employee and how and when the employee should update the manager.

- The manager also asks the employee about the employee's expectations of the manager. What does the employee need in order to perform at his or her highest level?

This last point may be surprising to some leaders, but setting expectations goes both ways. It is a mutual exercise. We can all see the obvious reasons for making our expectations clear to our people. However, it is equally important to ask people about their expectations of us. Ask your staff directly:

- What do you expect of me as a leader?

- How do you like to be managed to be your best?

- In your experience, tell me about the best boss you ever had. What made the relationship work for you?

- Tell me about the worst boss you ever had and what made it not work for you?

Get interested in the people who report to you. Learn in detail what makes them perform at their very best. People deeply appreciate this type of interest. Don't you? Even as a senior leader, don't you enjoy working for people who are not only clear with you, but also interested in how you like to operate? Setting clear expectations builds the foundation for mutual respect.

Example of an Expectation-setting Conversation

Sometimes executives and managers ask me what this "expectation-setting" conversation would actually sound like. For example, what if you have already been working with your direct reports for a long time? How and when do you have this meeting? The conversation below is an example. Remember: make these conversations natural and easy. Use your own style.

Susan is the Vice President: "the manager." Joe is the Director, her direct report: "the employee."

Susan: Hi, Joe. Well, as I mentioned at our last staff meeting, I am meeting with each member of my team to clarify each of our roles and expectations. As we discussed in the meeting, even though we've all worked together awhile, I think we have a stronger team when each of us is clear on our role and we also know other team members' roles. Make sense?

Joe: Sure.

Susan: OK, great, so why don't you summarize for me how you see your role as Director of Customer Service?

Joe: OK. Here's a one-page summary of how I see my role, as you asked each of us to prepare. I see these five bullets as the scope of my job.

Susan: Looks good, Joe! I agree with everything here. Now Joe, I would add one expectation not noted here: I also see you as supporting marketing in large customer presentations. How do you see that?

Joe: Well, Susan, I do attend sales pitch meetings when I have time, but those marketing guys just give away the farm anyway, so I stopped going. Why bother? The marketing guys are always selling things we can't service without added expense.

Susan: Good point, Joe. You're right. And that's all the more reason for you to get involved. This is an issue that goes directly to our profit margin. So I really would like you to make it a part of your role and see what you can do to get Marketing on the same page with you. Are you up to the challenge?

Joe: Will you back me when I need to say no to Marketing for business reasons?

Susan: Yes, as long as you can make a case. Marketing gets a shot at making their case too, though.

Joe: OK, then I will add that to my summary of my role. We'll play it out.

Susan: Also, Joe, I've never formally asked you: how do you best like to be managed? I think we do pretty well, but what more do you need job? More training? More information? Anything?

Joe: Overall, things are fine. But I could use more updates from the quarterly meetings you have with the CEO. I like to know more of the future direction exactly as the CEO sees it, in detail.

Susan: OK, agreed. I can do that. Sounds like we're on the same page.

Joe: Great, thanks!

"From the beginning, especially with newer people, I go through the whole strategy, the whole plan. We look at what the goal is and when we need this to be a reality. Even if I sound like a broken record, I repeat what we're doing. I don't repeat it in the same words so I sound like their mother or their teacher. I rephrase it...but I let them know.

"People learn differently. Sometimes I explain the expectations and people shake their heads, yes, yes. But sometimes they just aren't asking their real questions, so I may have to show them what I expect. Later I follow up to be sure they are clear on what we are doing."

— *Bob Mazza*
Manager, Safilo

New Market Conditions – New Expectations

So let's say you have clarified your expectations with your direct reports. Great. But how often do you have an additional conversation because your market place has changed? Many executives miss this important task. They assume that everyone knows the new pressures, new priorities, and so they must know the new expectations. Not true.

Even very senior people often see the new market conditions but continue to operate under old expectations. This is why so many corporate professionals feel so stressed. How often have you heard people say: "Things are changing at work so fast, I can't keep up." What they are often experiencing is the pressure they feel when they are trying to do what they used to do in a changed environment with new variables.

In summary, they have not updated their strategy for successful performance. It is a good leader's responsibility to be that catalyst, that reminder to people that when the big picture changes, we have to change with it. Leaders who do this routinely get far better performance out of their direct reports— particularly when the direct reports are at the vice president or director levels.

This is because as executives themselves, vice presidents and directors depend heavily on a clear understanding of the big picture. Executives at this team. They get things done through their peers. Therefore, when a CEO updates expectations with an executive team frequently (at least once a quarter), the payoff is significant. Imagine if every level of management had a quarterly staff meeting devoted for only one hour to updating:

- How the market has changed

- How customers have changed

- Changes needed to existing products and services

- Overall strategy for leaders

This type of regular expectation setting—both in groups and individually, changes a group of people from working side by side in silos to working together like a well-oiled machine.

Manager's Action Plan

- How many of the actions for setting clear expectations have you completed for each staff member?

- What action do you need to take to be sure every member of your staff has clear expectations?

- How do you actually know that each staff member understands expectations? What have you done to check their understanding?

STEP 2

GIVE FREQUENT FEEDBACK

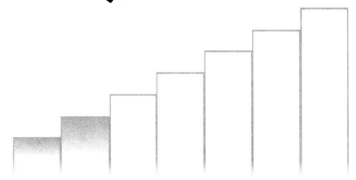

"I've often heard it said that feedback is 'the breakfast of champions.' What you are doing with consistent, balanced feedback is creating an agreement with your employees as to how you perceive their performance, both the good and what needs improvement. You are opening a dialogue for discussion. The employees are jazzed to see that what they do right is noticed and appreciated. And they have the opportunity to discuss obstacles with you, their boss, who is responsible for supporting them."

— Ana More
former Director of Sales *AT&T Wireless*

Once staff members are working, they will need feedback on their performance regularly. The goal of feedback is to change behavior and continually improve performance. Many managers say they are too busy to give frequent feedback. It is true that developing people requires an initial investment of time. However, the payoff is that people will soon perform at a higher level and more independently. Then the manager's job actually becomes easier and the manager will have more time.

The Three Rules for Feedback

There are three basic rules about feedback. Feedback to staff should be:

- Immediate

- Specific

- Face-to-face (whenever possible) and private

This means that the manager's job includes giving short feedback messages to staff regularly.

- Feedback on an employee's performance should be given immediately. We are all busy, but in order to improve performance, you'll need to coach staff on what they did as soon as it happens. This helps you prevent problems at the annual performance evaluation. There should be no surprises at the end of the year. If an employee is surprised in a performance evaluation, it is usually an indicator that he or she did not receive clear feedback along the way.

- Feedback needs to be specific. That means you tell the employee exactly what you observed in his behavior. Example: "The report was due last week and you turned it in four days late." Feedback is observed behavio r, not the manager's interpretation. Example: An interpretation of the prev ious example would be, " You are not committed to your job because your report was late." Feedback is summarizing what you actually saw, not your opinion of the reasons for what you saw.

- Feedback is best when it is face to face so that the manager can really interact with the employee and give her a chance to respond. If a face-to-face meeting is not possible, calling on the phone is the next best alternative. Memos and email are not good vehicles for feedback, since they are not interactive and do not convey enough tone and inflection. Feedback should be given in private.

- Generally, the more feedback you give people, the easier it is for them to change their behavior (if they are willing). Feedback is like the instrument readings that help an airplane stay on course. As a manager, you should go out of your way to deliver positive feedback, even on small items. This is what will balance the stage for the times when you have to give negative feedback.

Example of Feedback Conversation

Most executives and managers say they actually do notice their employee's behavior but they are too rushed to have a meeting to give feedback. You don't always need a formal meeting, especially when the feedback is positive. Example: John is the Chief Information Officer, the manager. Henry is the Vice President of New E Products, John's direct report, the subordinate. John and Henry just got off the same train, coincidentally, and are walking for ten minutes to the office together.

John: Hey, Henry! Nice job you did on the presentation of new products at our customer meeting last week; especially how you gave them the mouse pads as gifts, which had the specs of all three new products. Good work.

Henry: Thanks, John. I was wondering if that was too sales-y, but I guess it worked OK. My staff worked hard to prepare the presentation. Now, if we could only develop a solution for that new problem the customer mentioned.

John: Your team was great at brainstorming during your last staff meeting I visited. So I have total faith that you'll create a solution for this customer problem. That's something you guys do really well. In fact, here's some feedback for you: the way you lead brainstorming sessions with your own staff;

I'd like to see you take that same lead with your peers in our staff meetings. I often ask for a volunteer to lead the brainstorming and usually someone else volunteers, not you. I'd like to see you do it. You'd be great.

Henry: OK, thanks John! Next meeting I will.

"It is to your own benefit as a leader to give people feedback. They combine your feedback with their own knowledge and use it to improve. They will actually create new ideas for the business."

— Lori Stark Manager Prudential

So in summary, giving feedback is a very simple leadership activity. It's so simple that leaders usually completely overlook the value of consistent feedback. Giving feedback is one of those big pay-off activities. A few words can shape someone's behavior for a long time. It's a way to exercise one of the more subtle powers of being a leader. Your words matter to your direct reports. You are often their reference point for knowing if they are doing a good job.

Imagine how easily you can build someone's confidence with a few words like "nice job" or "great presentation." Imagine how helpful you can be to a direct report when you give feedback that tweaks good performance into excellent performance. For example, it takes only a few minutes to share with a subordinate: "Here's what I really liked about the report you did. It was well written, crystal clear, and summed up the company's present situation. I'd like to add a suggestion: Your recommendation at the end of the report was a little tentative. You said it would be up to senior management to decide on the new system. I'd like to see you make your own strong recommendation and outline all your reasoning. You are experienced enough to make your own case and advise senior management. I want to see you stick your neck out and risk taking a very clear stand."

Even short, simple feedback can bring out the best in your people.

Manager's Action Plan

- Think of the past week: To how many of your staff did you give unplanned, spontaneous feedback? Have you given both positive and corrective feedback as appropriate?

- How consistently do you meet the three rules of feedback?

- What changes do you need to make in your own behavior so that managers reporting to you learn to deliver feedback effectively to their own staff?

27

STEP 3

USE THE DEVELOPMENTAL CONVERSATION

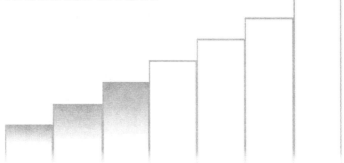

"Just be direct, honest and fair. In the end, people want the truth, even if it isn't the outcome they would have hoped. Trying to sugarcoat or delay giving feedback just causes both the manager and employee issues in the future. My experience has been that tough feedback, given in a timely and direct way, is better received and more appreciated."

— Andrea Ferrara
Director of Human Resources
Pepsi

Almost all managers and executives eventually feel the need to "have a talk" with one of their direct reports. There are several reasons. For example, you reach that point where your direct report may be doing an OK job, but she is just not rising to the occasion. You intuitively know she could be doing more, performing better. Or as another example, your direct report is actually letting the team down. He is performing below expectations and you can see the impact on the business and on the other team members. Or as a more positive example of needing to "have a talk," you have a superstar performer. She is doing great. But you can see she is not really challenged, sometimes bored, and you owe it to her to coach her to grow to her own next level of performance. Whatever the performance of your person, you can as the leader, use the "developmental conversation" to raise the bar.

The developmental conversation is an important tool for changing staff behavior. This conversation is broader and more planned than spontaneous feedback. Developmental conversations are equally useful for managing poor performers and for further developing good performers.

- Follow the seven-point structure of the developmental conversation (see Guidelines: Developmental Conversation).

- This conversation can be documented for the manager's own file. If necessary, a copy of the document can also be put in the official employee file.

- This conversation should be viewed as a "coaching conversation." The manager's role is to be a coach, a resource. Listening is critical so that you find out more about what will motivate your employee.

- Do not underestimate the power of the developmental conversation to solve almost any performance issue you have.

The developmental conversation is especially useful for higher-level direct reports. At senior levels (e.g., director reporting to a vice president), the conversation is actually closer to an executive coaching session. Although the conversation is pleasant and even collegial, a lot of development work is being accomplished.

Guidelines:

THE DEVELOPMENTAL CONVERSATION

These guidelines are presented to show the structure and content of the developmental conversation. However, the language the manager uses, and the style, should be adapted to the manager's personal style.

1. Preparation

- Meeting should be scheduled in advance, not "on the fly."

- Opening: "We are here to discuss your performance."

2. Employee Perspective

- Ask the employee, "How do you feel you're doing?" Letting the employee speak first helps to reduce defensiveness.

- Mirror understanding by paraphrasing what the employee has said. This builds rapport with the employee and demonstrates respect.

3. Present your Feedback

- Strengths (What has the employee done well?)

- Areas for development (What specific areas of performance are of concern?)

- Use observations, not interpretations. Example: "I have not been receiving your weekly report due on Thursdays."

4. Offer Assistance

- Ask, "Are there resources you need to help you with these areas for development?"

- Listen to the employee's response, and be prepared to follow through on getting the resources needed. As you listen for ways to help the employee, you are playing the role of coach.

5. Make Requests

- State specific behaviors you want to see. This is key. Ask for specific performance, such as: "I'd like to receive your weekly report by 5:00 p.m. every Thursday."

- Outline what resources are available to help the employee.

- Clarify when you would like the employee to report project status to you and what form the feedback should take.

- Discuss consequences of performance, both positive and negative.

6. Wait for Agreement

- Ask if the employee can make an agreement with you to fulfill the requests. If he or she cannot say yes, repeat step 4. Explore possible confusion, concerns and conflicting goals.

7. Next Steps

- Ask the employee to summarize. You need to hear the employee's view of this conversation. Also agree on next steps, such as: When will the employee update you? When is the next review of performance?

- It is wise to follow up a week later just briefly to see how the employee has performed. Although this follow-up should be brief, it is vital to demonstrating your commitment to the employee's progress and success.

Example of a Developmental Conversation

A developmental conversation does need to cover the points outlined in the guidelines. However, it can still be a flexible, natural and brief conversation. For example:

Stan is the Vice President of Operations (the manager). Joyce is the Manager of New Business Administration, his direct report (the employee).

Stan: Hi, Joyce. You know that every so often I like to touch base with each of you to see how things are going in general. So even though we don't have our performance evaluations for several months, I want us to talk about your role, how you're performing and whatever we need to plan for the future. You know my priority as a leader is to continually coach all of my people to be the best you can be. And I want to do whatever I can to support you.

Joyce: Yes Stan, I have heard you say that.

Stan: So, first Joyce, how do you feel you're doing as manager of New Business Administration? Why don't you briefly outline for me what you feel you do well and any areas you are working to strengthen?

Joyce: Well, Stan, I thought about that in preparation for this meeting. I'd say my top three strengths are 1) setting up new business on time, based

35

on our 90% customer satisfaction rate, 2) accuracy, based on 98% quality rating, and 3) my own team's satisfaction based on the recent positive employee survey. The only area I'm working on is to improve our set-up time from five days to three days. We can do it faster.

Stan: I would agree Joyce, that you are great at meeting deadlines and quality. And overall, your people seem satisfied since they get higher bonuses tied to the quality rating. So you are very strong in those areas. You are right. However, I'd like to give you some additional feedback on other areas.

Joyce: Sure. Is something missing?

Stan: Well, here's another area I've been observing: your interaction with your peers in other departments. How would you say you are doing with them?

Joyce: Fine. I do my job. They do theirs. I don't have that much interaction. I don't even see them that much. Is there a problem?

Stan: I agree with you. Technically, there's not a need for a lot of interaction. And I wouldn't say it's a problem today—but maybe a missed opportunity. What I observe is that you do not include your peers in any of your meetings. When we have projects, you do your own piece separate from your peers and you don't appear to collaborate much. Your peers say they don't know you and are not clear on all the roles of your department.

Joyce: Well Stan, I'm busy. I'm not here to be buddies with people. I get the job done. I don't believe in all that social schmoozing.

Stan: Well, no need to be best friends with your peers, but here's the question: You said your goal is to reduce set-up time from five days to three days. In order to do that, you will need your peers to also go above and beyond to deliver things to you faster. Right?

Joyce: Well, yes.

Stan: So, if you collaborated with them more, what impact might it have on your own success?

Joyce: Look, Stan, if they don't do their job, I'll just tell you (laugh). Hmmm...OK, I see what you're getting at. OK, I concede, they might be more cooperative if I worked with them more closely.

Stan: As you move up in the organization, your relationships and your ability to influence will become more and more important.

Joyce: I'm not good at small talk.

Stan: I can give you some tips on that. And it's not just about small talk. It's about influence. Here's my request: I'd like you to go to the "Influence Training" course next month. I'd also like to see you collaborating more with your peers. Can you agree to that?

Joyce: OK. OK.

Stan: Well, I'd like you to do it willingly, not "under protest."

Joyce: No, really, I get it. What you're seeing is that I'm just not sure I'll be good at it.

Stan: Then when that comes up, let's talk about it. Joyce: OK, that's fair.

Stan: All right, then what are our next steps?

Joyce: I'll sign up for the "Influence Training" next month and I'll start inviting the other departments to my meetings. I'll look for specific ways to collaborate.

Stan: Great! When will you update me?

Joyce: In two weeks, I'll email you an update on where I am.

Stan: Great.

Let's put the developmental conversation into perspective. This is a conversation to help a person "develop" into what he or she can be. It is not necessarily punitive or negative when we have to take someone aside for a talk. It is very similar to sports when an athletic coach calls a player out of the game who is not performing at the highest level. Coaches often tell the player, "Get your head in the game!" Or coaches give the player a pep talk that creates a new, big-picture perspective for how the player is performing. The player then goes back into the game with a new opportunity to play at a higher level.

So as leaders, we need to be on the lookout every day. Who needs that pep talk? Whose head is not in the game? The developmental conversation is intended as a useful, positive catalyst.

However, there will be times when, even after this developmental conversation, an employee does not change her performance. In that case, it is totally appropriate and necessary to take the progressive discipline route. This may lead to the employee being terminated or asked to resign.

Leaders should have no guilt about this if it unfolds this way. In short, the leader needs to be certain that they have made expectations clear, that they have given regular feedback, that they have had several developmental conversations and that they have followed their company's progressive discipline guidelines. If all that has been done (and done well), and the employee does not change, then the employee has terminated himself. In the long run, when an employee is performing poorly, it is usually best for both the company and for the employee to separate.

In that way, the employee can move into another job that better matches his ability and interests. We don't do anybody a favor by trying to avoid termination when termination is actually the best solution.

Generally, developmental conversations work to keep direct reports performing at a high level. However, as leaders, we have to be prepared that it could go either way, depending on the employee.

Manager's Action Plan

- How skilled are you at going through all seven points of the developmental conversation?

- Do you have at least two developmental conversations a year with each of your direct reports (in addition to their performance evaluation)?

- Are you satisfied that you are using developmental conversations to effectively coach your people? What evidence have you seen that your conversations change staff performance?

STEP 4

GIVE A POWERFUL PERFORMANCE EVALUATION

"Giving an honest and thorough performance review is vital to employees. This feedback lets each employee know the supervisor's view of his or her performance, provides a forum for employees to discuss their perception of their own progress, and gives both the supervisor and employee the opportunity to map a development path for the employee together. I have given many performance reviews to employees globally, and regardless of cultural background, the feedback was welcomed. It is a strong learning tool for employees everywhere."

– Sandra Beach Lin
President,
Alcoa Closure Systems International

Many managers view performance evaluation time as a burden. However, the performance evaluation is a primary tool for leveraging your power as a manager. When used effectively, the performance evaluation can shape an employee's behavior for a very long time. This is as true for an employee who is at supervisor level as it is for one who is a vice president.

If your employees are not performing the way you would like, ask yourself if you could be more effective in your evaluation of their performance. Performance management is a critical leadership skill for managers to develop.

Some basic points for giving a powerful performance evaluation:

- The annual performance evaluation is in many ways just a more expanded developmental conversation (prior chapter). The points to cover in the actual discussion of performance are the same as the seven points in the development conversation (see "Guidelines: Developmental Conversation").

- It is useful to ask the employee to give you, in advance, a written summary of his or her annual performance from their own viewpoint. Suggest a simple, brief format that includes:
  ◊ Recap of the employee's beginning-of-year objectives
  ◊ Summary of results on each objective
  ◊ Specific strengths the employee demonstrated this year

◊ Areas the employee wants to strengthen for his or her own professional development

- The annual performance evaluation should summarize observations of behavior for a full 12 months, not just recent performance. As always, the written comments should be specific observations of performance, not interpretations.

- A good performance evaluation should present no surprises to the person being evaluated. It should be a summary of feedback you have given all year. If you find yourself wanting to write about an area for improvement but you have never given feedback to the person before, it should not be in the written evaluation. You never gave the person an opportunity to improve.

- The power of the performance evaluation is in how you as the manager present the big picture. In addition to the guidelines previously presented for the development conversation, also remember to:

  ◊ Consider the complete picture of the employee's performance: positive and negative.

  ◊ Be unconditionally constructive in your language.

  ◊ Paint a picture of the employee's future. If he continues performing at his current level, what will the consequences be? If he raises his level of performance, how different will his future be?

◊ What can you say/do to inspire improved performance? How can you mentor/coach most effectively? Ask for your employee's input.

"When managers have employees who are not meeting their expectations, my experience has shown that it always, always boils down to one thing. COMMUNICATION! People don't open their mouths and speak to one another. Communica te your expec ta tions!! In a performance evaluation, we must tell the truth. Tell them what they have been doing right so they can keep doing it and perhaps do it even better. Then tell them specifically what they have been doing wrong so they have an opportunity for a 'light bulb' moment and they won't do it again. That's it. It's actually very simple."

– Mihlee Robinson
Director,
Human Resources Village Voice

Maryanne's Story

"I first learned how important it is to do a good performance evaluation from my personal experience with my boss, who did not know how to handle performance evaluations. I was a fairly high-level manager at the time. My boss was an engineering director. I had always received stellar evaluations before working for him. When he gave me my annual evaluation, it was largely positive but one dimension: 'written communication' was rated 'less than satisfactory.' I was shocked! I had never received a less-than-satisfactory rating in my entire career. He said it was related to the technical writing I was doing as part of a monthly status report.

"Well, then I was really angry. I had given him these reports for several months and not once had he given me any feedback at all. Not a word. Apparently, he had rewritten some of my reports himself, but he never told me.

"This was one of those moments in a career where I felt that this was so unfair that I was willing to take a stand no matter what the cost. I told my boss: 'You never gave me one comment on my writing skills over the last several months. You effectively cheated me out of any chance to improve. It was your responsibility to tell me if I needed to make changes. You did not. So I will not accept criticism now on my written performance evaluation. In my whole career, I have never felt the need to take an issue to Human Resources, especially as a manager, but if we have to go there now together, I'm ready.' I was angry, disappointed in him as a boss and ready to fight.

"My boss was stunned by my assertive stance. He sheepishly and immediately changed the 'less than satisfactory' rating to 'satisfactory.' And over the next few weeks, he started giving me the feedback he should have given me all along on changes I could make to my technical writing. So my performance evaluation and management bonus turned out fine. But I lost all respect for my boss as a leader. I learned how important it is to give my own staff feedback all year long, and then nothing in the annual performance evaluation is new or a surprise."

Ken's Story

"I've been a manager my whole career, most recently a vice president of a financial services company. My direct reports are vice presidents and leaders in their own right, so I have learned some things about evaluating high-level and high-performing people.

"Most of us are so busy we don't look forward to doing mid-year or annual performance evaluations. You just don't ever have the time. I found ways over the years to make it easier and faster for myself. Essentially, I pay attention every week to my direct reports' performance.

"I keep my own private, unofficial folders, one for each direct report. On a daily basis, when they do something under the heading of leadership skills, positive or not, I throw my quick handwritten note, or a copy of their email into their folder. It takes five seconds. Then every few weeks I quickly scan the folder to be sure I've given regular feedback. By the time the annual performance evaluation comes around, I simply take out my folders and I already have all the specific behavioral examples I need to write the performance evaluation quickly. I don't have to rely on memory.

"Then, when I present the evaluation, I can focus more on motivating and coaching my direct report to develop their strengths, particularly leadership skills. They tend to trust my suggestions since they know I have been paying attention to their development all year long.

"What I've learned is that when our direct reports are high achievers and self-motivated, they are looking for our mentoring and coaching. So it's helpful to have specific examples of their performance to illustrate both their current strengths and ways they could be even stronger.

"I've come to the point now where, as a manager, I can write performance evaluations easily and I actually enjoy the one-on-one conversation as I review the evaluation with my direct report."

Manager's Action Plan

- Rate yourself on a scale of 1 to 10. 10 means you are a master at giving powerful performance evaluations and your staff knows it. How do you rate? Which skills do you need to improve?

- Ask your staff for feedback. How would they assess your skill at performance management? For best results, be sure to elicit their honest assessment.

- A key indicator for managers is how well they meet deadlines for giving performance evaluations. We tend to procrastinate on tasks we are not completely comfortable with or confident about. How many evaluations did you present on time or early? How often did you delay a performance evaluation?

STEP 5

PRACTICE THE ART OF TRUE DELEGATION

"I give my people the opportunity to fail. I challenge them until they are put to the test. They get to know what they are capable of very quickly; and I get to know what they are capable of. It creates an independent atmosphere for them and for me. Usually, everyone comes through.

"But even if they fail, we sit down and go over what happened in this assignment. Then we give them the tools they need to succeed. And we go on from there."

– Glenn A. MacFarlane
Vice President,
Insurance Finance and Planning TIAA-CREF

True delegation is an art, not a science. Delegation is often viewed by managers as simply telling a staff member to do a task. However, delegation is much more than that. When used correctly, delegation can be the backbone of how a manager truly trains and develops people.

The very first step of delegation is one that managers often overlook. The first thing a manager should do when considering a task is to ask two critical questions.

1. Should this task be done? Here, the manager needs to weigh the current workload, priorities and resources. Managers often assume that whatever is presented to them needs to be done and their job is to find a way to do it. However, a true sign of leadership is to make the decision whether or not the task should be done at all and in what time frame. How does it fit into the big picture?

2. The second question is then who should do the task? This is also a part of leadership. Who does a task has a big impact on the outcome. Notice that the "who" is not necessarily the leader. In fact, usually not.

• Before delegating a task, the manager should know: Why am I giving this task to this person? Is it just because it falls under her scope of responsibility? Or, can I evaluate this employee's skills by how well she does this particular task? Which specific skills am I evaluating? Will this task be a challenge or a routine activity for this staff member?

- At the time of delegation, the manager should make clear to the staff member:
  ◊ What specific deliverable is expected from this task?
  ◊ In what format does the manager want to see the deliverable?
  ◊ What is the deadline?
  ◊ How frequently and in what way does the manager want to be updated?
  ◊ How far can the staff member go? What are the limits of his authority for this particular task?

- The manager should ask the staff member:
  ◊ What obstacles might be expected?
  ◊ What resources might be needed?
  ◊ How does this task fit in with your other priorities?
  ◊ How confident are you that you can complete the task on time?

- Key issues the manager should assess:
  ◊ How does doing this particular task challenge the staff member to go beyond his previous level of performance?
  ◊ Does the task need to be expanded or cut down to match the staff member's level of skill?

The idea is to use every act of delegation as an opportunity, as an exercise to push the employee's performance to new heights. This is what empowers employees to have greater and more complex levels of responsibility. The key is to match well each time you delegate, so that the task is one step above the employee's current skill set.

Managers frequently do not delegate enough because:

- They feel they can do the task better themselves.

- They feel the staff member is not experienced enough to handle the task.

- They fear that if the staff member makes a mistake, it will reflect poorly on them as the manager.

All of these reasons are understandable, but it's important not to let them become obstacles.

- Managers who want to do everything themselves are only stunting their own growth. By holding onto tasks, they prevent themselves from having the time and free attention to exercise the higher-level management skills of strategic planning, creating a vision for the organization's future and ensuring that staff members have the resources they need. Such managers will prevent their own promotion. In fact, when managers feel they have to do tasks themselves, and not delegate, they are not just preventing their own promotion; they are almost giving themselves a demotion. They are returning to lower-level activities instead of staying with higher-level leadership activities.

In addition, managers who do tasks themselves are actually cheating their staff out of an opportunity to grow. Staff members need the delegation of tasks so that they learn new skills. Your job as a leader is to coach them through this growth—not prevent their growth by denying them the chance.

"My first manager used to say to me, 'Trust the system. If the system is broken, we will fix the system. Performing tasks yourself that are better done by others prolongs the life of a broken system.'"

— John Redmond
Senior Vice President
of a major insurance brokerage firm

- If you feel a staff member is inexperienced, that in no way has to stop delegation. It just means you must be more thoughtful about which parts of the task to delegate. Delegate the parts of the task that match the employee's experience and add something slightly above her level of experience. Gradually, staff members should be given more and more responsibility. That is exactly how they gain practical experience.

This is where the "art" of delegation comes in. As the leader, you will need to become good at assessing your people's exact level of competence. That's how you'll know what tasks to give them and when to request that they do more. You'll also have to decide exactly how much of your guidance they will need during a specific task and what it will take from you to be sure they have the best chance to succeed. This assessment is part of the leader's role.

- If a manager is concerned that a staff member may make a mistake, this is a signal that the manager must consider how to use deadlines. The manager should give the staff person an earlier deadline so that the manager has enough time to review the deliverable, coach the employee, and have the employee do the revisions before the final deadline.

- Each time the employee gives updates on the deliverable, the manager can use that interaction as an opportunity to give feedback. What was done well? What needs work?

"Valuable lesson on delegation—It's important for both the manager and the report because it al lows each person to grow and develop. Managers must be willing to 'let go,' allowing reports to build confidence in their efficacy/ abilities, blossom, 'figure it out,' and have the opportunity to lead efforts and make decisions. If this doesn't happen, the team, project and environment become sterile and stagnant."

– Jewel Love
Vice President
MEE Productions Inc.

Tony's Story

"I'm the Director of Information Systems of a major men's clothing company. I have four systems managers who report to me, one for each major business unit of the company. Delegation is not so easy in my type of work. There are huge consequences if an installation fails. We could cost the company millions in lost revenue if the sales people can't access the system to do their jobs.

"So I admit I did not want to delegate. I got promoted quickly because I was the guy who did the systems applications fast and right. I'm good at it. Frankly, I inherited my four direct reports. I couldn't be absolutely sure they were as quick or knowledgeable as I am. I had to learn to delegate the hard way. Our company is only 10 years old and we have doubled in size in the last two years. I was doing as much as

I could myself but the sheer volume of work was beyond what I could do. Then I noticed I was getting up at 4:00 a.m. to do email so I could be at the office by dawn and work until 8:00 p.m. I knew I was going down the wrong path. But it took that level of pain before I started delegating more to my guys.

"It's been about six months now that I have been delegating and it hasn't been easy. Any time they make a mistake or they take longer than I would, I have to take a deep breath. I have to remind myself that they are gaining skill every day. I am now able to get out of the office at a decent hour about twice a week. I'm also actually looking ahead to our strategy for the next two years. So I'm not sure if this delegation thing is a growth experience more for my direct reports...or for me!"

"The easiest aspect of delegation is doing it. The hardest part is providing a learning opportunity for the person you delegate to."

— Joyce Robinson
Credit Analyst
Kraft Foods

Manager's Action Plan

- How thoughtful and thorough are you in planning how to delegate tasks?

- Are you satisfied that you delegate enough to everyone?

- Does your delegation continually provide opportunities to improve staff performance?

- How satisfied are you that, as a leader, you are spending enough time on higher-level skills, such as creating a vision, planning and leading vs. doing tasks yourself?

STEP 6

USE COACHING SKILLS
TO MOTIVATE

"If you have to invoke your power, you have really lost the game. It comes down to the definition of a manager vs. leader. Managers get people to do things. Leaders get people to 'want' to do things."

– Alan Adler, M.D., M.S.
Medical Director
Horizon Mercy Health Plan

As managers, we do not actually motivate employees. Employees motivate themselves. However, the manager's job is to create the environment that is most conducive for employees to feel motivated. One way to create an inspiring environment is to use coaching skills when interacting with employees.

As a foundation for developing good coaching skills, managers should ask themselves a key question: "How do I relate to people in a way that helps them shift their perspective and improve their performance?" Good coaching is about action. Good coaching means that an employee's performance and behavior actually change.

Sometimes leaders follow the initial steps we have discussed in earlier chapters. They set clear expectations, they give feedback, they have a developmental conversation when needed, they delegate. However, at this point in the process, some leaders fall down on the job. They think, "Hey, I clearly set you on the path and gave you some feedback, so now you are on your own. Let me know when you complete the trip." Some leaders don't stick around for the ride with their people or support them along the way. Coaching skills are the tools for supporting your people during the ride, along the way.

Key Coaching Skills

There are hundreds of good coaching skills, but here are six fundamental skills every manager will find useful.

- Listening "with"

- Making people right

- Handling conflict

- Sharing your intuition

- Requesting

- Coaching questions

Each of these coaching skills is best developed with specific training and follow-up practice; however, here is a brief overview of each skill.

Coaching Skill: Listening "with"

Listening "with" a person is a higher level of listening than just listening "to" them. Listening "with" means being a partner with the person, listening for what is not said, listening for deeper messages, and listening for the broader context. For example: Why is this person telling me this particular story now? What else is he trying to express beyond the obvious? What is he expressing that maybe he himself is unaware of? The goal is for the manager and subordinate to listen together to what the subordinate communicates.

A New Leader's Story

This is an example of how a leader who was new to a team started by just listening.

"The most valuable lesson I learned is to recognize and use the experience of my staff. Some years back, while a member of management with a large insurance company, I took over a team that had been through quite a bit of change. I gathered everyone in a room and allowed them to list all the things they would change if they could. As a group, we then prioritized the issues according to the impact they had on the staff 's ability to effectively do their jobs.

"The next step was to assign the top ten issues to individuals who would research and develop possible solutions, which would then be presented to the group. After the group came to a consensus on next steps, someone from the group would volunteer to take ownership for the implementation of the next steps.

"This process was incredibly successful. Rather than having a group of people complaining and venting about how things were out of their control, we had people stepping forward to take on various assignments to find solutions.

Bridges were built with other departments that had previously been seen as adversaries, work-arounds were developed for problems which required longer-term solutions, and the morale and produc tivity of the group dramatically increased.

"Also, rather than being seen as an outsider who had to prove herself, I was immediately embraced by the group as a team member and resource. Leading this group was a joy. Because I listened to them and valued their input, they were supportive of my decisions even when those decisions took them outside their comfort zone."

— Carol Newlin Searles
former Director

Coaching Skill: Making people right

The most practical reason to make people feel right is that when people are made to feel wrong, they become defensive. Then communication usually stops. Making people right means looking for the ways, from their point of view and under their assumptions, that they are right. It is truly stepping into their viewpoint, not a condescending "allowing them to think they are right." When managers are secure, they can handle this temporary change in perspective.

This does not prevent the manager from correcting the person, but correction is done after making them right. For example: "Yes, you're right, John; when you look at it from X, Y, Z. Here's another perspective to consider: When you look at it from A, B, C, we could do it this way. What do you think?" When people feel

---

they are acknowledged first, they are usually more open to being influenced to a new point of view.

Donna's Story

"Ray was the best boss I ever had. I did a great job for him. Yes, I was totally motivated. Why? Well, I'd like to be able to tell you that Ray had all these great techniques or that he was such a technical genius. But it wasn't that.

"Ray was a real person and we felt he cared about us. He was happy. He smiled. He asked us about our lives. Ray told funny stories about his kids. He wanted to know about our kids. He was really engaged with us at staff meetings. He let us totally disagree with him and then he would sell us on his approach.

"We felt he respected our individuality. Maybe it was because he was a salesman before he was an executive. He never relied on his authority as the boss. He always tried to 'close the sale' with you, convince you of the value of his strategy. And he was good at it.

"When he transferred to a new division we were pretty upset. Later, when he left the company for a better job, some of us actually cried. And

---

during the next year, several of us left the company too. It just wasn't the same without Ray. That motivation was gone."

Coaching Skill: Handling conflict

Handling conflict is essentially an expansion of the skill of making people right. The first thing for the manager to "get" is that conflict is not bad. Conflict is one of the many parts of being human. The key is how conflict is managed.

Using this positive perspective as a backdrop, conflict can be handled well with a practical, step- by-step conflict resolution model (see Guidelines: Conflict Resolution Model).

"Most people view the world differently from you. Expect it. It's normal."

— Greg Meyer
Executive Coach

Guidelines:

CONFLICT RESOLUTION MODEL

1. Preparation
   - Meeting should be scheduled in advance, not "on the fly." Requesting a mutually convenient time demonstrates respect.

2. Present your concern
   - Present your view of the conflict in neutral language. State the observable facts, not your interpretations. Example (a conversation with a peer): "My boss told me that you complained to him that I didn't give you the report you requested. However, I never got any message from you that the report was overdue, so I was disappointed that you went to my boss without saying anything to me."
   - Ask for the other person's view without any assumptions about their behavior. Example: "What happened?"

3. Listen until you experience the other side
   - Listen "with" the person. Listen until you actually can experience their viewpoint. That means going beyond their words to try to understand their point of view when they made their decision.

4. Restate what you heard

- Summarize what you heard the person express. This does not mean you agree. You are demonstrating that you are clear on what they said. Example: "OK, so you're saying that you called my boss because you heard that I was out of the office for the day. Do I have that right?"

5. Present your viewpoint

- Now share how you feel about the situation. Do not accuse or judge the person with statements like "You did X, You should have done Y." Instead, use "I" statements. Share how you feel. Example: "I felt disappointed that you didn't at least leave me a voicemail so that I could try to get you the report myself."

6. Respectfully request

- Now that you have shared your point of view, what do you want the other person to do? What is your request? Making a specific request is usually much more useful than blaming or rehashing what happened. Example: "May I make a request? Next time, would you agree to either leave me a voicemail or send me an email to give me the opportunity to help you before contacting my boss directly? I often check messages even when I'm not in my office." Wait for the other person's agreement. If you don't get that agreement, keep talking until you do. Discuss further if the agreement needs to be revised.

After the meeting, take a few minutes to reflect on the discussion. What did you learn? What caused the conflict? Could you do anything differently next time? Conflict always presents the opportunity for a learning experience.

Example of Conflict Resolution Conversation

Deb is the Vice President of New Business Administration. Frank is the Vice President of Human Resources. They are peers who both report to the same Senior Vice President, Tom. The conflict is that Deb has complained to Tom that Frank is an obstacle, slowing down Deb's ability to set up new business more quickly. Their boss, Tom, has asked the two of them to work it out. (Frank is following the conflict resolution guidelines.)

Frank: Hey, Deb. I assume you saw Tom's email that you and I should meet. When are you available? I can do it any day except Thursday.

Deb: Uh, yeah. OK. Let's meet. How about tomorrow at 9?

Frank: OK, I'll come to your office then.

Next day at 9 a.m.:

Frank: Well, Deb, I know we don't have much time, so I'll get right to the point. Tom told me that you said Human Resources is an obstacle for you; that you feel we are the reason you can't get new business cases set up faster. I guess I want to understand from you what your concerns are. I know our direct reports have had meetings with each other from time to time, but I didn't know it was so serious.

Deb: Well, it's more than serious. We are at a total impasse. My director has dealt with three of your people with no results. Look, Frank, we are under a lot of pressure from the sales guys. They are selling 700 new business cases a month and that means my staff has to grow to meet the demand. We call Human Resources to get new hires, and we get a song and dance about a 12-week lead time to get a body in here. We don't have 12 weeks. The cases are here now. Your people just recite the rules to us.

Frank: OK, so you are saying that the lead time we need to hire new staff is too long for you? Is that right?

Deb: Absolutely. How hard can it be to get an entry-level professional in here? This is a well-paying job in a new business with a career track.

Frank: OK, I get the urgency. I've dealt with the sales guys, too. Maybe we haven't done a good job of explaining what's happening in that 12- week lead time. We are going through a lot of pre-screening, drug testing, interviewing. I thought you needed a very specific profile for the new business set-up job. We are not trying to be obstacles in HR. We are trying to get you the best possible employees.

Deb: Well, OK, that's fine, but we don't have to have a perfect process, just an effective one. Here's an idea: What would it take to cut the lead time from 12 weeks to six weeks? What would we have to live without?

Frank: Wow! Cut the time in half? OK, well, let's see... it means HR would probably have to be part of your planning meetings. Then instead of waiting for your actual request for staff, we could anticipate based on what we hear in your weekly planning staff meeting. So that would save lead time. But even with that, we would still have to skip some steps. We may not be able to do the upfront background check. It means we would move the candidate to you sooner but you would risk the possibility of making the offer to hire them and having the background check come back negative.

Deb: Hey, we are willing to risk that. The percentage of background checks that are a problem is pretty small for a job at this level, right?

Frank: Yes, that's true.

Deb: And no problem having HR join our weekly planning meetings.

Frank: OK. Well, with those changes, we can definitely get the lead time down to eight weeks. Let's try it and then we'll look for what else can be eliminated to get to six weeks. Agreed?

Deb: OK, agreed. Let's try it. Hey, Frank, let's meet again next week to see how it's going, OK?

Frank: OK. Thanks. We'll get it done.

Coaching Skill: Sharing your intuition

Sharing your intuition is sharing your gut feeling. What does your gut say is really going on with the person in front of you? We often hesitate to share our gut feelings out of fear of being incorrect. However, there is a good reason for you as a manager to share this intuition, even if you are wrong: it can still move the other person forward. For example: The manager says, "John, I think the problem is X." If the manager has truly created good rapport and an open environment, John is likely to either confirm that statement or to say, "No, it's not actually X, it's Y." So, even in the latter case, the manager gets more information and possibly the solution to the problem. The manager gave the person something to react to versus nothing.

73

"Each day I make it my goal to go to each person and say, 'Good morning.' I look in their face and get an impression of how they are. I can tell how they are feeling by looking in their eyes. If I feel they are out of integrity with themselves, they will be out of integrity with their work. It is my duty to pull them aside and have a conversation with them. When people are allowed to share how they are feeling it not only empowers them, it empowers me also. We can stop being stuck in our own private conversation."

– Gene Pascucci,
DDS Owner, dental business

Coaching Skill: Requesting

Requesting is a simple skill, but one that is often over-looked. When managers are coaching employees to learn new behaviors, the manager can be helpful to the employee by requesting that the employee demonstrate the behavior.

Requesting, like delegation, is an art. What specific thing should you request the employee to do that will challenge her ability? Sometimes the employee will exceed the manager's expectations. Therefore, it is important for managers to make big requests so that employees stretch. If the employee fails, the manager should be there to help her learn from the experience and try again.

"One of our administrators is excellent at the skill of making requests clearly and directly. She is very pleasant...but she never goes away!"

— Karen Peterson
Associate Professor of Nutrition
Harvard School of Public Health

Coaching Skill: Coaching questions

Coaching questions are questions that shift and motivate a person. These questions contain a message to the person without lecturing him. Some examples:

- What is next for you?

- What are you willing to do about that?

- What is missing for you?

- What do you most want for you?

- How much longer will it be before you make some real changes?

Doug's Story

"I run the claim operation area of an insurance company. We have over 500 staff and their six managers report to me. So this whole idea that I need to 'coach' my people doesn't really seem practical to me. We have real-life problems that need to be solved today. We get angry phone calls from people wanting payment and we have a lot of work to move out of the door. I don't have time to sit down and have a nice warm and fuzzy chat with my people. We have to get the work done.

"But I do have to say that when we had our training class on 'coaching skills for managers,' one particular coaching skill has been useful to me: Asking coaching questions. I notice that it makes my life a lot easier when I ask questions to get my managers to think for themselves instead of me just barking out the orders.

"For example, the other day one of my managers came to me complaining for the one-hundredth time that he doesn't have enough staff to manage his workload. And now that I'm listening better, I finally really see that he himself is part of the problem. He tells me it's turnover, that he can't get people to do a claims job very long and then it takes eight to ten weeks to get a replacement. I usually tell him what to do to handle the immediate workflow crisis. But this time I used questions. I asked him, 'What's really missing in this whole picture that causes you to keep having this problem?' He actually stopped talking and thought about it. He admitted he's so busy he doesn't have time to look at the big picture. I used the same coaching questions we had in the class. I asked him, 'What are you willing to do about that?' and finally 'How much longer before you make some real changes?' He stopped complaining and said he realized he needed to make a strategy once and for all. We decided to have a follow-up meeting next week for him (not me) to present a plan.

"So, as a busy executive, I may not be 'coaching' all the time, but I use the particular skills that make my life easier."

Big Picture of Coaching Skills

When you look at coaching skills from a big-picture perspective, it all adds up to this: A strong leader is a strong coach. A strong leader coaches individual team members and also coaches the total team. Here is a good way to capsulize how a strong leader coaches the total team:

"In my view, a leader has three major areas of accountability. The only things that a leader can effectively do to produce performance in an organization are these three.

"First, the leader is responsible to PROVIDE DIRECTION to the organization. Of the three kinds of accountability, this is the most visible, and in many ways, the most direct. The leader must provide the direction through unambiguous messages (i.e., JFK: We're going to land on the moon by the end of the decade), so that a clear beacon is in place when members of the team are struggling with conflict and an ambiguous environment. If the direction is clear, the priorities become clear.

"Second, the leader is responsible to PRODUCE ALIGNMENT throughout the organization. Of the three areas of accountability, this is the most indirect and probably the most difficult. Once the direction is in place and clear, the task of aligning the organization to execute crisply is challenging. In command and control organizations, alignment is produced by the hierarchy. However, in many of today's distributed, high-performance organiza-tions, where diverse viewpoints are welcomed and encouraged, the task is far more difficult. It is the leader's job to produce organizational alignment in the midst of conflicting views and parochial agendas. Although many times the alignment task is through direct, one-on-one discussion between the leader and the team member, frequently the leader must create the alignment conversation indirectly, in the absence of his/her own participation. For example, the leader, in a behind-the-scenes role, may need to

orchestrate a discussion between two or three team members that results in a fully aligned strategy to execute the leader's direction. This approach, though more challenging and usually more time consuming , frequently results in organizational alignment that is stronger, more sustainable and more resistant to conflict and environmental cross-currents.

"Third, the leader is responsible to ENABLE PERFORMANCE throughout the organization. This type of accountability comes in many forms, including training, tools, communication forums, and even 'flying air cover' for teams on the front line engaged in the 'hand-to-hand combat' of organizational business."

– David Samuel
General Manager
IBM Global Energy & Utilities Industry

Manager's Action Plan

- Take a look at the Key Coaching Skills. Rate yourself on how effective you feel you are with each skill.

- Which skill do you need to practice more?

- On a scale of 1 to 10, 10 being the highest, how well do you manage conflict? What gets in the way of your managing conflict?

STEP

WALK THE TALK

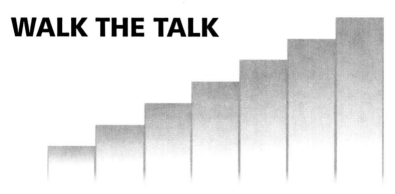

"As a leader, it is important to present yourself in a positive light. It actually helps people when you do that. When people ask me, 'How are you?' I respond, 'Excellent.' It makes people think about themselves. It makes people ask themselves, 'Why is he excellent?'"

– John Locke
Manager
Schering-Plough

Leadership is about inspiration. People tend to follow people who inspire them. If you want to get the best out of people in the real world, you have to give them a reason to want to listen to you. That means you will have to walk the talk, practice what you preach.

It is often said, "If you want to teach someone something, just demonstrate it." Developing people is coaching people. It's leading people. It's inspiring them to be the best version of who they can be. In order for people to know that this is possible, they need to see you being the best version of you that you can be.

Think of any complaint you have about your employees. For example: "They're not independent enough." Then check your own behavior to be sure you are modeling outstanding independent leadership. Example: If they are not independent enough, are you delegating enough? Delegation provides the vehicle for staff members to develop key skills they will use in becoming more independent. Are you making big enough requests? If your staff is not creative enough, are you listening to their ideas enough? Are you clear enough in your expectations? If your employees seem to repeat the same mistakes, are you giving them adequate feedback? Are you using developmental conversations?

Learn to use your employee's overall performance as a mirror for your overall management. Where can you stretch your leadership? Are you getting feedback from your staff? What are your own strengths and weaknesses? To get the best out of people who work for you, you also have to get the best out of yourself. Are you walking your talk?

Let's cut to the chase on this subject of "walking the talk." Most of us agree that it means we need to do what we tell our staff to do. We need to behave in a way that is consistent with our words. All of that is true.

But there is a deeper level of walking the talk that executives and managers almost never look at seriously. That deeper level is this: The question is not what are you doing at work. The question is who are you being at work. Walking the talk means you are being the person that you truly value being.

The Corporate Mask

For example, many of us feel that corporate America is a cold place. We say that we have to be impersonal and tough in order to survive in such a harsh, corporate environment. On one level there is certainly truth to this. But who is making the rules about how to be? Who said the only way to survive is to bury your emotions, be totally impersonal and have a poker face while you recite the corporate policy? As individuals, we say: "I'm really not like that. I'm actually a warm person, but I can't be that way at work. I have to be professional." Really? Who says? Those of us who are or have been senior executives: we are the leaders. We create the culture.

If we don't feel there is room for being human, who will? We are in charge.

So the real "walking the talk" means taking the risk to BE REAL with people; and still be an outstanding leader. It means integrating who you are as a human being with all your executive skills for running a business. It means letting down the corporate mask and connecting with the people who report to you. Not in a "syrupy sweet, nice guy" way, just in a real way. It means showing people who you are and what you believe in and asking the same of them. It means being equally comfortable with yourself when you are promoting a staff member or terminating a staff member. Because if you truly "walk the talk," you are consistently straight with people and your actions come as no surprise.

Appreciation

Another aspect of walking the talk is actively showing your people appreciation and recognition. As leaders we often say that people are our greatest resource. When we give speeches to "rally the troops," we talk about how the organization would not be successful without our people. But do you actually demonstrate that appreciation on a daily basis? Really? How?

"Let your staff shine. Give them credit—publicly—for a job well done. Step way back and watch them enjoy the spotlight."

— Kathy Gulrich
Artist (previously Managing Director and
Creative Director for advertising agencies in
New York and abroad)

One key lesson I have learned through years of managing and coaching people is this: People want acknowledgement. They want other things, too. People want money, they want exciting and meaningful work, they want a great environment! But those things never take the place of acknowledgement.

As a leader, a major part of our job is still that management principle of MBWA (Management by Walking Around). Nothing replaces occasionally walking up to a direct report's desk to recognize him for something he did well. Or, if you are geographically dispersed, send an email of recognition to the whole team when the team has a success, no matter how small.

Appreciation is one of the best motivators a leader can offer people, and it doesn't cost anything. Appreciation means that you, as a leader, extend your attention and energy to someone and value their contribution. Many executives and managers overlook this important leadership skill. They say they are too busy and they will remember to mention it at the next performance evaluation. But appreciation, like all feedback, is most powerful when it is immediate and tied to specific behavior. People feel appreciation at a deep level and it helps them further develop their skills.

We, as executives, know this intuitively through our own personal experience. Haven't you noticed that the higher the level executive you are, the less appreciated you personally feel?

Senior vice presidents and chief executive officers do get the compensation and other perks of their jobs. However, they often do not get daily appreciation for the challenges they struggle with. At higher levels, it is more difficult even to articulate what your work is. So the daily building blocks under a CEO's success can often go unnoticed and unrecognized. In short, people at all levels in the organization need to be reminded of what they do well and how it adds value.

Showing appreciation and recognition is a significant way to walk the talk of leadership, and it brings the best out of your people.

Manager's Action Plan

- Whatareyourfivemajorvaluesasaleader? What do you believe in?

- For each value, how do you specifically demonstrate it on a daily basis? How do you walk the talk?

- Do your people know that you appreciate them? How do you show them?

SUMMARY

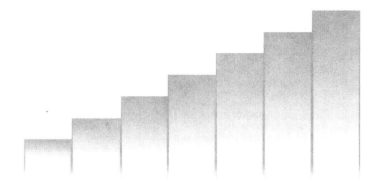

Now you have the 7 Practical Steps for developing top performance. There are many additional things you can do to develop people successfully, but these are fundamental. The steps are a checklist, the actions you want to make sure you are taking to get the best out of your people.

Periodically you can rate yourself and evaluate, "How well do I develop people?" To do this, look at the 7 Practical Steps in a big-picture way and rate yourself on a scale from 1 to 10:

1. How clearly and frequently do I state my expectations to my direct reports?

2. How often do I give my people feedback, positive and corrective?

89

3. How many times a month am I having <u>developmental coaching conversations</u> with my direct reports?

4. Do I use <u>performance evaluations</u> as a powerful tool to change behavior all year long?

5. How effective am I at tailoring <u>delegation</u> to match my staff's need for challenge and experience?

6. How skilled a <u>coach</u> am I?

7. Do I <u>demonstrate</u> the high level of performance I want from others?

How satisfied are you with your own performance of these seven key skills?

Why Bother?

Some senior executives might say: "Why bother with these 7 Steps to get the best out of people? Why have another thing to think about?" And especially if the organization is profitable: "Why work with your people in this deliberate way?"

Because it matters. The obvious reason is that it will make your job as a leader easier. But it matters in other ways. As most of us have noticed, life in a corporate America is not great these days. Corporate America is in trouble and needs to be fixed. Why are so many of the best and brightest people quitting their corporate jobs? Many start their own businesses. Many leave the business world altogether in search of a more meaningful, balanced life. Corporate America cannot afford to continually lose so much talent. Who will be left to lead? To innovate? To take risks?

That's why it matters that we manage people in a better way, that we work to bring out their best and our best. Because that will make corporate America a better place to work.

It's time for all of us to play a bigger game.

As an Executive Coach, I am interested in how you actually use these ideas in your daily life to make your job easier.

Let me know!

Email Val Williams at:
val@valwilliams.com

Website: www.valwilliams.com

About the Author

Val Williams is an Executive Leadership Consultant and Master Certified Coach who runs her own business: Influential Presence, LLC. Val presents training seminars to organizations and also coaches senior executive leaders individually to achieve career and personal goals. She specializes in Leadership, Presence and Influence.

Val's experience includes several years as a Managed Health Care Executive at Prudential Insurance, managing staffs as large as 700 people. Val was Executive Director of Prucare, the HMO of Northern New Jersey; Director of Prucare Customer Service Operations for the Northeast Region; and Director of Group Underwriting, Prucare of New York. Val has managed an annual operating budget of over 25 million dollars with direct impact on a network of 500,000 insured patients and 8,000 physicians and hospital providers.

During her 13 years' experience at Prudential, Val managed several other areas, including Financial Services, Facilities Planning and Field Office Lease Negotiations.

Prior to her corporate career, Val worked with people on both physical and psychological rehab. Val earned a Bachelor of Science from Tufts University and a Master's Degree in Counseling Psychology from Boston University.

People throughout the United States, France, Finland, England and Japan have worked with Val to raise the quality of their leadership. Val coaches people (often by telephone) to develop greater focus and overcome obstacles so they design the life they really want. In her seminars, Val is known for her interactive approach and practical style.

As a Coach, Val has presented seminars and coached executives at a variety of corporations, universities and professional organizations, including: Blue Cross, General Electric, Prudential, National Utility Investors, TIAA-CREF, American Express, Genentech, Pfizer, Harvard University, Pepsi, Nokia, University of Indianapolis, Horizon-Mercy HMO, Delta Dental, American Heart Association, Schering-Plough, ADP, Raytheon, in different formats: either individual coaching for executives or group coaching for senior executive teams.

Val has been credentialed and awarded the designation "Master Certified Coach" by the International Coaching Federation.

See Val's website: www.valwilliams.com.

Val is also the author of several leadership books:

- *Executive Think Time: Thinking That Gets Results*

- *Executive Foundation: 5 Essential Skills for Senior Leaders*

- *Virtual Leadership: Great Tips for Managing People From Afar Using Today's Technology*

- *Get the Best Out of Your People and Yourself: 7 Practical Steps for Top Performance*

- *Butterfly Coaching: A Leadership Tool for Developing People*

- *The Influence Puzzle: 6 Aspects of Powerful Executive Presence*

Share It With Others

If you'd like to order more copies of this book or any of our other books for your team or for colleagues:

Please visit our website: www.valwilliams.com or Amazon.com.

(For large order special discounts: contact Val directly at val@valwilliams.com)

CPSIA information can be obtained at www.ICGtesting.com
Printed in the USA
BVOW01s2257161013

333940BV00008B/119/P